EVERYDAY MIRAC~

Unleash the miracle power ~~
welcome everyday miracle.
33 impactful archangel pray,
embrace and absorb their love
connect with them.

INSPIRATION

Get inspired through seven true stories of ordinary
people who receive angelic assistance to solve their
pressing problems. And believe, without a doubt,
that you can do the same.

DIVINE BEAUTY

Step through life-changing portals into heavenly
realms with 33 fine-art angel paintings by Marius
Michael-George and feel the profound emotions
shared by those touched by these angelic master-
pieces.

FREE GIFTS

Broaden your perspective and spark new insights
with our offering of seven small gifts, which you
can access online at bit.ly/mysevengifts.

Welcome to the world of the archangels.

Enjoy!

THE
MIRACLE POWER
OF THE
ARCHANGELS

**A NEW WAY TO FULFILL YOUR DREAMS
BY EASILY TAPPING INTO DIVINE HELP**

GEORGE MAKRIS

WITH 33 PAINTINGS BY MARIUS MICHAEL-GEORGE

HOUSE OF THE ARCHANGELS

THE MIRACLE POWER OF THE ARCHANGELS
A New Way to Fulfill Your Dreams
by Easily Tapping into Divine Help

by George Makris

ISBN 979-8-9896606-0-5

Disclaimer: The author and this book, including the additional content recommended as small gifts, do not provide medical advice or endorse any particular method as a means of treating physical, emotional, or medical issues without the guidance of qualified medical professionals, either directly or indirectly. The author and publisher's intention is solely to present general knowledge for informational purposes only. No guarantee is made that the spiritual practices described in this book and additional content will produce positive outcomes for anyone at any time. Never postpone seeking professional advice or treatment in the fields of physical or mental health, finance, or law because of what you read in this book. If you choose to apply any information from this book for yourself or others, the author and publisher assume no responsibility for your actions and will have no liability.

Note: The names, locations and minor circumstances of individuals described in the stories have been changed to protect their privacy.

Printed in the United States of America

CONTENTS

INTRODUCTION

The archangels are spiritual beings of great power who stand ready to give their loving assistance to each of us, our families and our communities.

Aside from the countless spiritual references affirming their reality and their service to humanity, we at the House of the Archangels have experienced their intercession in our personal lives many times.

And we strongly believe that as more people start placing their attention upon the archangels and enlisting their aid, they can overcome their greatest challenges, receive blessings of hope, love and joy and even witness miracles.

That is why our mission is to spread greater awareness of these majestic beings and bring them into the lives of millions.

We strive to facilitate this divine exchange through our offerings of angelic fine art, books, products and more. The 33 powerful archangel prayers in this book are part of this effort.

By unleashing the miracle power of the archangels through the archangel prayer that you need most at any moment, you can be sure that divine help will appear.

Now is the time to let go of all doubt and limitation and seize the opportunity to receive angelic support.

We wish you the best and look forward to connecting with you soon.

George Makris & Marius Michael-George
Founders, House of the Archangels, Inc.

P.S. Check out our website at
HouseOfTheArchangels.com
and drop us a note. We would love to hear from you.

CHAPTER 1:
TWELVE INTRODUCTORY
QUESTIONS AND ANSWERS

QUICK PRAYER:

Blessed archangels, come into my life today!

The miracle power of the archangels is their ability to enter our lives and offer divine assistance in the form of protection, healing, guidance, transformation and much more. This miracle power is one of the greatest untapped resources available to us today, and all we need to do to access it is call upon the archangels and ask them for help.

Below are twelve questions and answers that will give you a better understanding of the archangels. The rest of the book will show you how to harness their miracle power to improve your life and the world.

What is an archangel?

An archangel is a leader, or captain, of vast legions of angels. *Arch* comes from the Greek word *archos*, meaning "chief, highest," or "most important." The last two letters that appear at the end of *archangel*, as well as each of the archangel's names, signify God—or *El*, in Hebrew. Archangels are to God what rays are to the sun. In other words, they are the stepped-down energies of the Presence of God sent to assist us. The archangels are honored in many spiritual paths and not limited to any particular religion.

Who are the seven archangels?

Though there may be numerous archangels in the spiritual world, the prayers in this book call upon seven of them: Michael, Jophiel, Chamuel, Gabriel, Raphael, Uriel and Zadkiel.

Do the archangels specialize in different areas of service?

Yes, they do. Just as we specialize in different professions, each archangel expresses a unique aspect of God's consciousness that relates to their area of service. While an archangel can answer any prayer, it's best to go to the right archangel for the right blessing when we need help. Understanding how to determine that is the aim of this book. For example, we ask Archangel Michael to protect us, Archangel Gabriel to give us hope, Archangel Zadkiel to help us forgive, and so on.

Am I worthy to receive the help and the blessings of the archangels?

Absolutely! As a child of God with a divine spark in your heart, you are loved. You are worthy. You are powerful. And you can receive the help of the archangels right now. You can be certain the archangels know you and care about you personally, and they are literally waiting for you to ask for their help.

Tell me again why I need the archangels in my life?

The archangels have tremendous spiritual capabilities—what we have termed their miracle power. As emanations of the Divine, their role is to serve as our guides, guardians and friends and to give us their blessings when we need them. We just have to ask. When we give an archangel prayer in a time of need, they receive our request immediately and will respond. Even if it is not in the way we might have expected, it is always in our best interest. Some people find that when they welcome the archangels into their lives, they feel inspired and uplifted.

Why can't I go directly to God?

You can. And it's a great practice to talk intimately with God at any time. As mentioned above, the archangels are extensions of God's energy and specialize in matters pertaining to our physical existence. It's important to understand that when asking the angels to help us, we always do so in God's name. (See Chapter 2 for more on how and why to request the intercession of the archangels in the name I AM THAT I AM.)

Why do I have to ask before the archangels will help me?

As human beings, we possess the gift of free will, which allows us to experiment with life, to learn from our actions and, ultimately, to grow spiritually. Within this spiritual framework, the archangels don't have the authority to infringe on our free will, even though they would love to help us purify our consciousness and improve our overall well-being. However, unless we make a conscious choice to ask them to assist us, or others who need a helping hand, they will not interfere in our lives.

Is there anything I need to do before giving an archangel prayer?

Dedicating a sacred space in your home to the archangels is a wonderful way to invite their energy into your prayer sessions. Before beginning, take a moment to breathe deeply to create a sense of inner calm and clarity. It's helpful to quiet your mind, center in your heart and send gratitude to the specific archangel you are working with. As you pray, trust the divine energy coming to you from the archangel, and accept its power to heal and transform you. At the same time, you can also visualize, feel and believe in the outcome that you wish to achieve, bringing it into your present reality.

Will the archangels grant me anything I want?

The archangels are not genies, though they are most willing to give us what we need when it serves our divine plan. They cannot be forced into action by human willfulness. Nor can they be summoned to grant us whimsical, unnecessary things that we ask for in moments of ignorance or selfishness. As we learn to work with the archangels, we come to understand that their role is to assist us with things that will bless us and others and further our soul evolution.

How much time does it take to receive blessings from the archangel prayers?

There's no definitive answer to this question. The archangels will respond to our requests for assistance when the divine timing is right. And that timing is often different from our human sense of timing.

How does the connection with the archangels feel?

Connecting with the archangels often engenders feelings of joy, oneness and bliss. Even if you don't experience a noticeable shift in feeling when calling upon them, you can be sure they have heard your prayer and are acting on your behalf. Certainly, beyond the blessings that they bring, drawing close to the archangels is its own reward.

How can I express my gratitude for the guidance and assistance of the archangels?

Everyone loves to be loved, including the archangels. So the simplest way to thank them is to send them pure love from your heart. You can also pause for a moment, allow the feeling of gratitude to fill your being and then send it to the archangels, as well as to anyone in your life. Sharing your knowledge of the archangels with others and encouraging them to explore their own connection to them is another way to express your gratitude. Most importantly, becoming the instrument of the archangels and radiating their energy and grace into a world in need is perhaps the greatest way you can honor them.

In conclusion, remember that nothing is impossible for the archangels. They transcend time and space and can do anything, as long as what we ask for doesn't hurt any part of life, is in accordance with our divine plan and is honorable.

All it takes is for us to invite them into our lives to reveal divine solutions to our human problems. That, in fact, is their purpose, and they are happy when some among us give them the green light to act in our world.

CHAPTER 2:
UNDERSTANDING
ARCHANGEL PRAYERS

QUICK PRAYER:

Seven Archangels of Light, help me now!

The goal of this book is to help people resolve their most pressing problems—one problem at a time—by teaching them how to unleash the miracle power of the archangels. A unique and effective way to unlock this power is by giving the prayers offered in these pages.

What will make these particular archangel prayers so powerful?

Giving them with love, gratitude and surrender.

Giving them not as a supplicant, but with the authority of the inner flame burning on the altar of your heart.

Giving them in the name of God, I AM THAT I AM.

A Simple Plan of Action

You can start by picking the most pressing issue in your life today. If you have difficulty isolating a problem, you can use the table of contents to choose something that strikes you as relevant to your current situation.

Once you've decided what you'd like to work on, read the chapter on the corresponding archangel and send them your love and gratitude. Familiarize yourself with the words of the prayer before giving it in earnest so that you can lessen the involvement of your mind and center in your heart.

Next, give the archangel prayer out loud in a resolute voice. A mumbled or routine prayer that you hardly pay attention to and don't put your heart into may barely receive a tangible response. On the other hand, a determined and heartfelt prayer has the potential to bring about a strong and sometimes immediate response. For inspiration, you may want to look at your favorite painting of the archangel while giving the prayer.

Continue to recite that prayer every day, until you feel a transformation taking place. If you are moved to do so, you can recite the prayer more than once a day, such as three or nine times.

The practice is simple, and you may be surprised at the results.

THE STRUCTURE OF ARCHANGEL PRAYERS

Each archangel prayer has seven parts:

1) Naming the archangel
2) Asking for the help of the archangel, in the name I AM THAT I AM, on an issue that you are facing
3) Being specific about what you would like to accomplish
4) Requesting daily guidance and support
5) Thanking the archangel
6) Accepting the blessing
7) Asking for the blessing to be multiplied for the benefit of all beings

To explain the seven steps in greater detail, we'll use the "Archangel Prayer to Find Peace" as an example.

Here's the prayer in its entirety:

Archangel Uriel, blessed Patron of Peace, servant of the Most High,

In the name I AM THAT I AM, I ask you to help me attain a state of serenity.

Enfold me in your wings of peace and enable me to master my emotions.

Vanquish all forces of anti-peace in my world, and empower me to find inner calm.

Teach me to respond to all challenges with equanimity and to not react when things don't go the way I expected.

Guide and support me each day.

I thank you for receiving my prayer and for your service to humanity.

And I accept the blessing of peace, in keeping with my divine plan.

This which I ask for myself, I ask for all beings on planet Earth.

Following is a breakdown of each of the seven steps:

1) Naming the archangel

Archangel Uriel, blessed Patron of Peace, servant of the Most High,

Here we address the archangel, acknowledging his role in the heavenly realm.

2) Asking for the help of the archangel, in the name I AM THAT I AM, on an issue you are facing.

In the name I AM THAT I AM, I ask you to help me attain a state of serenity.

Because each of us has a divine spark in our heart, we have the power and authority to call upon the archangels in God's name, I AM THAT I AM. This was the name that God revealed to Moses in the Old Testament story of the burning bush (Exodus 3:14). Many spiritual devotees of varying traditions understand that when we say "I AM," it affirms that the infinite nature of God resides within the sacred temple of our being. It is from this place that we speak with authority. It is from this place that we summon the miracle power of the archangels so we can receive their intercession and blessings in our lives.

3) Being specific about what you would like to accomplish

Enfold me in your wings of peace and enable me to master my emotions.

Vanquish all forces of anti-peace in my world, and empower me to find inner calm.

Teach me to respond to all challenges with equanimity and to not react when things don't go the way I expected.

The more specific our prayers to the archangels, the more specific their responses will be. It's no different than our human requests to one another. The same commonsense principles apply to spiritual affairs.

4) Requesting daily guidance and support
Guide and support me each day.

Beyond asking the archangel to solve the particular problem we are facing today, we also request their ongoing guidance and support.

5) Thanking the archangel
I thank you for receiving my prayer and for your service to humanity.

It's a natural human instinct to thank people who show us kindness and graciously meet our needs, large and small. So it's only polite to do the same with the archangels. In addition, the more we sincerely give our gratitude to the archangels, the closer they will come to us.

6) Accepting the blessing

And I accept the blessing of peace, in keeping with my divine plan.

Even when a blessing is granted, we may sometimes subconsciously reject it. Affirming our acceptance of the blessing allows us to set aside our subconscious blocks and open ourselves to receive it.

7) Asking for the blessing to be multiplied for the benefit all beings

This which I ask for myself, I ask for all beings on planet Earth.

Since the power of the archangels is limitless, we want to take this opportunity to help others while we are helping ourselves. Put differently, we welcome the prospect of being the chalice of the archangels through which they can pour their great light into the world and make it a better place.

As we conclude this chapter, remember this: The miracle power of the archangels is an antidote to negativity and the many challenges that we all face. May you embrace the archangels, who stand ready to release this power, and allow them to help you claim a better life for yourself and all whom you hold dear.

CHAPTER 3:
ARCHANGEL MICHAEL,
OUR GREAT PROTECTOR

ARCHANGEL:	Michael
MEANING OF NAME:	"Who is like God"
MAIN ROLE:	Great Protector
SYMBOL:	Sword
COLOR:	Blue

CALL UPON THE MIRACLE POWER OF ARCHANGEL MICHAEL TO:

- Receive divine protection
- Build self-confidence
- Find the perfect job
- Have a great day
- Conquer fear

QUICK PRAYER:

Archangel Michael, protect me right now!

INTRODUCTION
TO ARCHANGEL MICHAEL

Archangel Michael is one of the most well-known and revered archangels. He is often depicted as a powerful warrior, standing tall and fierce, with a sword in hand and a shield by his side.

If ever there was a heavenly being to make friends with, especially in times of trouble, it is Archangel Michael. Mentioned in several spiritual traditions, he is often seen as a messenger of God, a protector of the faithful and a guide for those who are lost. He is also the protector of the innocent, the defender of the righteous and the vanquisher of evil.

Known as the Prince of the Archangels, he holds a high rank in the hierarchy of heaven as leader of the angelic hosts. His name means "Who is like God."

Served by untold legions of angels, he is dedicated to protecting us and our loved ones from harm. We can appeal to him for guidance in our hour of need and ask him to stand up for us when we are being wronged.

Learning to work with Archangel Michael, who radiates a fiery electric-blue light, can change our life in profound and dramatic ways. No matter how dire the situation, reaching out to him is bound to bring a divine solution. It may not be exactly what we expect, but it will be the best one for us from the perspective of heaven.

Many people report having been miraculously protected by Archangel Michael. Stories like the one that follows are common.

TRUE STORY:
SAVED FROM A TUNNEL PILEUP

Susan studied hard at New York University, where she took nursing classes. So when her friends invited her along for a hike at a nearby mountain one early fall morning, she couldn't have been happier.

Her friend Ben was to pick her up from her dorm. Susan knew that he believed in Archangel Michael. "We need protection in busy traffic," he would always say. But Susan never took him seriously and even laughed at him. We don't need protection for a short trip across town, she would think to herself.

This time was no different. As soon as Susan got into the car, Ben gave his prayers aloud to Archangel Michael.

Minutes later, Ben's Prius entered a tunnel, and before anyone realized what was going on, Ben slammed on the brakes. The five friends jolted forward in their seatbelts.

A deafening noise of crashing metal and shattering glass pierced their ears.

Susan managed to catch her breath and open the door. At least thirty cars and trucks had collided, both in front of them and behind them, causing a serious pileup.

But Ben's car was untouched. It sat like a solitary island in the midst of the pileup, with six feet of clear space all around it.

From then on, Susan asked Archangel Michael to protect her anywhere she went—even for a short trip across town.

ARCHANGEL MICHAEL IN OUR LIFE

Archangel Michael is our Great Protector. He brings us the gifts of courage, guidance and determination and helps us overcome all obstacles that may come our way. When we invite this great archangel into our lives, we discover faith as a shining star that dispels the darkness of the night, showing us the way ahead.

As human beings who strive to grow emotionally and spiritually, it's natural to feel vulnerable and uncertain at times. When faced with challenges, we may be tempted to shrink back and hide from our problems. We may even get angry at God for allowing such seeming injustices to happen to us.

Although a sense of powerlessness may be hard to resist, it's not something we should hold on to. We simply can't continue to beat ourselves up, feeling miserable and overwhelmed. It's not just unhealthy—it doesn't work.

Ultimately, we must learn to meet our struggles and harness the power of determination and faith to overcome them.

And that is when we need to call to Archangel Michael, the Great Protector, to come to our side. To place before us his shield of light and keep us safe from harm. To cut away all negative thoughts with his flaming sword. To bring us into his divine embrace, where we are loved and secure.

Archangel Michael's assistance is not the same as the temporary solutions—or distractions—we often seek. His intercession is a steady and unwavering source of support that's always available to us, whether we recognize it or not. All we have to do is ask.

So let us feel the peace and security that come from knowing we are loved and protected at all times, and uplift those around us with the same courage and determination that we receive.

May we become vessels of angelic protection, shielding those in need and inspiring others to do the same, even as we work together to create a world built on love, hope and goodwill for all.

PAINTINGS

To see these paintings in color, please go to
<u>HouseOfTheArchangels.com</u>

FIRST SMALL GIFT:
FROM NEGATIVE SELF-TALK
TO EMPOWERMENT

How many times a day does the average person say to themselves, or to those around them, "I am tired," "I am poor," or even "I am such a loser"? If we counted the times, we would probably be shocked.

Because our words and thoughts have the power to shape our daily reality, especially when fueled by strong emotions, we may unwittingly be engaging in this kind of self-sabotaging behavior.

Your first small gift will show you a new method to make your words serve you rather than undermine you, with the help of Archangel Michael. This new method is deceptively simple and easy to apply, yet powerful at the same time. To instantly access your gift, please visit our website at the URL below:

<u>bit.ly/mysevengifts</u>

ARCHANGEL PRAYER
TO RECEIVE DIVINE PROTECTION

Archangel Michael, blessed Great Protector of all who seek your aid, servant of the Most High,

In the name I AM THAT I AM, I ask you to protect me and my loved ones.

Place your mighty blue shield before me and guard me from all harm.

Wield your sword of light and set me free from all obstacles before me.

Teach me to release all negativity and to be strong when I face life's challenges.

Guide and support me each day.

I thank you for receiving my prayer and for your service to humanity.

And I accept the blessing of protection, in keeping with my divine plan.

This which I ask for myself, I ask for all beings on planet Earth.

ARCHANGEL PRAYER TO CONQUER FEAR

Archangel Michael, blessed Great Protector of all who seek your aid, servant of the Most High,

In the name I AM THAT I AM, I ask you to help me conquer fear, especially _____.

Place your mighty blue shield before me and fill me with your divine faith.

Dispel all shadows of doubt and make me fearless.

Teach me to be strong when I face danger and uncertainty.

Guide and support me each day.

I thank you for receiving my prayer and for your service to humanity.

And I accept the blessing of conquering my fear, in keeping with my divine plan.

This which I ask for myself, I ask for all beings on planet Earth.

ARCHANGEL PRAYER
TO BUILD SELF-CONFIDENCE

Archangel Michael, blessed Great Protector of all who seek your aid, servant of the Most High,

In the name I AM THAT I AM, I ask you to help me build my self-confidence.

Place your mighty blue shield before me and give me the courage I need to stand in the world as a self-assured person.

Liberate me from the shackles of doubt, self-criticism and fear of judgment, and empower me to fearlessly shine my light into the world.

Teach me how to step into my power and how to use it wisely.

Guide and support me each day.

I thank you for receiving my prayer and for your service to humanity.

And I accept the blessing of greater self-confidence, in keeping with my divine plan.

This which I ask for myself, I ask for all beings on planet Earth.

ARCHANGEL PRAYER TO FIND THE PERFECT JOB

Archangel Michael, blessed Great Protector of all who seek your aid, servant of the Most High,

In the name I AM THAT I AM, I ask you to help me find the perfect job as soon as possible.

Place your mighty blue shield before me and take command of my career.

Dissolve all limiting beliefs that may be blocking my discovery of the perfect job that aligns with my abilities and divine purpose, and that will bring me happiness, fulfillment and abundance.

Teach me to express my very best self and make a difference wherever I work.

Guide and support me each day.

I thank you for receiving my prayer and for your service to humanity.

And I accept the blessing of finding the perfect job, in keeping with my divine plan.

This which I ask for myself, I ask for all beings on planet Earth.

ARCHANGEL PRAYER
TO HAVE A GREAT DAY

Archangel Michael, blessed Great Protector of all who seek your aid, servant of the Most High,

In the name I AM THAT I AM, I ask you to help me have a great day today.

Place your mighty blue shield before me and be with me wherever I go.

Deliver me from all negativity and fill my heart with joy, love and peace.

Teach me to recognize all opportunities that come my way and how to make the best choices.

Guide and support me each day.

I thank you for receiving my prayer and for your service to humanity.

And I accept the blessing of having a great day today, in keeping with my divine plan.

This which I ask for myself, I ask for all beings on planet Earth.

How People Experience Our Angelic Fine Art

"These paintings take my breath away. They open doorways into the beauty and healing harmonies of the higher realms, places I have only glimpsed in my dreams. They have the power to transform though the eye, as Beethoven through the ear."

—*Geraldine*

"These prints are simply out of this world. They are life-changing portals into the heavenly realms!"

—*Sandra*

"This art is a gift to the world. I have the image of Archangel Michael and his powerful sword on my mantle to remind me of the wisdom and light within."

—*Robin*

"I simply love your angels. I love especially Archangel Michael, as he is a great help to me when I ask him for it."

—*Elizabeth*

"This art is stunning. It adorns almost every room in our home! No words can fully convey how I feel when I look at these paintings."

—*Denis*

CHAPTER 4:
ARCHANGEL JOPHIEL,
OUR WISE TEACHER

ARCHANGEL:	Jophiel
MEANING OF NAME:	"Beauty of God"
MAIN ROLE:	Wise Teacher
SYMBOL:	Torch
COLOR:	Golden yellow

CALL UPON THE MIRACLE POWER OF ARCHANGEL JOPHIEL TO:

- Gain wisdom
- Reinforce positive thinking
- Strengthen self-worth
- Overcome adversity
- Achieve success

QUICK PRAYER:

Archangel Jophiel, flood me with wisdom right now!

INTRODUCTION
TO ARCHANGEL JOPHIEL

Archangel Jophiel, whose name means "Beauty of God," is a beloved figure among spiritual seekers, known for bestowing his wisdom upon those who desire it. He is also seen as a guardian of the righteous and a defender of those who are working to bring light and love into the world.

Archangel Jophiel is often depicted holding a torch of illumination or a book of knowledge, symbolizing his role as a source of enlightenment and understanding. He emits a golden-yellow light that can bring us insight and clarity as we navigate through puzzling situations. And he is the perfect one to call upon to help us access our Higher Self—our personal source of all things beautiful and holy.

Many people believe that calling upon Archangel Jophiel can help us improve memory, increase concentration and enhance creative thinking. He also removes the veil of ignorance that often covers our minds and he encourages us to listen to our inner directions as we make our way through life.

Jophiel is believed to have been the guardian of the tree of the knowledge of good and evil in the Garden of Eden. What's more, together with Zadkiel, he is considered to be one of the two standard-bearers who follow directly behind Archangel Michael as he enters the battle against the fallen angels.

TRUE STORY:
TRUSTING THE ANGELS BRINGS ABUNDANCE

Robert owned a small car-repair business in Minneapolis, Minnesota. Lately, he had invested in new equipment, which forced him to look for ways to cut costs and increase profits.

One day, a retired elderly woman came to his storefront and asked if he had any openings for a front-desk secretary. Robert hesitated because he couldn't afford to pay for another employee. "It made no sense for me to hire Lottie at that point," he said. "But I just couldn't reject her outright."

Robert was torn. On one hand, he didn't want to turn away someone in need of work. But on the other hand, he didn't want to invest the extra money. He knew he had to make a tough choice.

Feeling overwhelmed and uncertain, Robert asked a spiritual friend for help. The friend advised him to first clear his mind, ask the angels for guidance and then trust whatever feeling came through.

Robert did as he was told and was prepared to wait for some sort of sign. Yet the response was immediate. An overwhelming feeling to hire Lottie flooded his heart. And even though he still thought it was a bad idea, he decided to take a chance and offered her the job.

Lottie thanked Robert and promptly declined his offer.

"I was stumped and thought Lottie was a little nutty," he said. "But when she explained that she had needed friends and not money, I understood." Since their first encounter, Lottie had arranged for two roommates to live in her house, giving her plenty of social time with friends.

Still, the two kept in touch, Lottie never forgetting that Robert was willing to hire her in her hour of need. After two years, just as suddenly as she had appeared in Robert's life, Lottie passed away.

In her will, Lottie left Robert her new Subaru and $25,000 in cash. Looking back, Robert felt grateful for the angels that helped him put aside his mind and follow his heart.

ARCHANGEL JOPHIEL IN OUR LIFE

Archangel Jophiel is our Wise Teacher. He grants us inspiration, illumination and deeper connection with the higher realms. He shows us things from a spiritual perspective and opens our minds to new possibilities. When we welcome Archangel Jophiel to join our spiritual journey, we learn that wisdom is like a compass that guides us through life, helping us to navigate its twists and turns.

With the complexity and information overload of today's world, we sometimes make the wrong choices. Without even realizing it, we may seek external validation or approval rather than trusting our inner guidance.

This inability to discern the best way forward can lead us down paths that don't align with our highest good, often causing confusion and frustration. What's more, we may struggle to take the next step needed to make positive change in our lives.

In the end, it is only by tapping into our deep inner wisdom that we can truly grow and flourish as individuals.

And that is where Archangel Jophiel, our Wise Teacher, comes in. We pray to him, in the name I AM THAT I AM, to flood our mind with illumination. To connect us with our inner wisdom. To help us discover the wise solution that we seek.

Archangel Jophiel's wisdom is not the kind of knowledge we can find in books. It is a higher, divine wisdom that comes from the consciousness of an archangel. It is a wisdom that banishes ignorance. It is a wisdom that connects us with our destiny.

May we each become a beacon of this divine wisdom, beaming our light upon all those we encounter, bringing greater clarity and understanding to ourselves and the world. Together, we can create a better tomorrow.

PAINTINGS

To see these paintings in color, please go to
<u>HouseOfTheArchangels.com</u>

SECOND SMALL GIFT:
THE GREATEST THEFT OF ALL AGES

The theft of our divine identity is the greatest theft of all ages. And that metaphorical theft has taken place because many unwitting parents and teachers did not tell us that we have a divine spark in our heart. Or that we are loved, worthy and powerful, without any preconditions.

As a result, throughout our lives we have experienced feelings of shame, inadequacy, anxiety and more. When we understand the nature of this theft and reclaim our stolen divine identity, we will finally be free to experience peace of mind, emotional healing and inner joy.

You may access your second small gift, *The Greatest Theft of All Ages,* by visiting our website at the URL below. The download includes a fable that you will always remember.

<u>bit.ly/mysevengifts</u>

ARCHANGEL PRAYER
TO GAIN WISDOM

Archangel Jophiel, blessed Wise Teacher, servant of the Most High,

In the name I AM THAT I AM, I ask you to help me receive divine wisdom.

Shine your torch of golden illumination upon me, and inspire clarity and insight in every area of my life.

Banish ignorance from my world and empower me to make the best and highest choices.

Teach me to have discrimination, and make me a source of wisdom to everyone I meet.

Guide and support me each day.

I thank you for receiving my prayer and for your service to humanity.

And I accept the blessing of wisdom, in keeping with my divine plan.

This which I ask for myself, I ask for all beings on planet Earth.

ARCHANGEL PRAYER
TO REINFORCE POSITIVE THINKING

Archangel Jophiel, blessed Wise Teacher, servant of the Most High,

In the name I AM THAT I AM, I ask you to reinforce my positive thinking.

Shine your torch of golden illumination upon me, and open my mind to a more optimistic outlook.

Lift the load of negativity from my shoulders and show me new possibilities.

Teach me to embrace a can-do attitude, and make me a steadfast positive force to all around me.

Guide and support me each day.

I thank you for receiving my prayer and for your service to humanity.

And I accept the blessing of positive thinking, in keeping with my divine plan.

This which I ask for myself, I ask for all beings on planet Earth.

ARCHANGEL PRAYER TO STRENGTHEN SELF-WORTH

Archangel Jophiel, blessed Wise Teacher, servant of the Most High,

In the name I AM THAT I AM, I ask you to strengthen my self-worth.

Shine your torch of golden illumination upon me and unveil to me my divine identity.

Release me from the bondage of poor self-worth, and empower me to give my unique gifts to the world.

Teach me that I am worthy because I am a child of God and not because of any outer accomplishments.

Guide and support me each day.

I thank you for receiving my prayer and for your service to humanity.

And I accept the blessing of greater self-worth, in keeping with my divine plan.

This which I ask for myself, I ask for all beings on planet Earth.

ARCHANGEL PRAYER
TO OVERCOME ADVERSITY

Archangel Jophiel, blessed Wise Teacher, servant of the Most High,

In the name I AM THAT I AM, I ask you to help me overcome adversity, especially _____.

Shine your torch of golden illumination upon me and show me how to navigate this hardship with determination and grace.

Clear the way before me and direct me toward the most practical and compassionate solution for all concerned.

Teach me the lessons behind this situation, and enable me to access my inner strength to meet future challenges.

Guide and support me each day.

I thank you for receiving my prayer and for your service to humanity.

And I accept the blessing of overcoming this adversity, in keeping with my divine plan.

This which I ask for myself, I ask for all beings on planet Earth.

ARCHANGEL PRAYER
TO ACHIEVE SUCCESS

Archangel Jophiel, blessed Wise Teacher, servant of the Most High,

In the name I AM THAT I AM, I ask you to help me achieve success in my life, especially in the area of

_____.

Shine your torch of golden illumination upon me and give my life an upward spin.

Remove all barriers from my path, especially self-doubt, and impart to me the vision and courage I need to fulfill my goals.

Teach me to be constant in my pursuit of success, even as I remain humble and kind toward others.

Guide and support me each day.

I thank you for receiving my prayer and for your service to humanity.

And I accept the blessing of success, in keeping with my divine plan.

This which I ask for myself, I ask for all beings on planet Earth.

How People Experience Our Angelic Fine Art

"Your paintings made me cry tears of joy to discover again and again that we are surrounded by the love of such divine beings. Thank you."
—*Mariangela*

"Beautiful divine paintings. I was at peace looking at these paintings. Light and love."
—*Esther*

"My young daughter loves her Archangel Jophiel, and the picture of Archangel Michael is a blessed gift for my unborn son. Thank you and many blessings."
—*Helen*

"Oh, such heavenly visions! This is the most beautiful sacred art I've ever seen! Love and light to you."
—*Angela*

"I was amazed by the unexpectedly beautiful and heartfelt art. How did you capture the beauty of the spiritual world? Your art shows the serenity, purity and kindness of God through the archangels."
—*James*

CHAPTER 5:
ARCHANGEL CHAMUEL,
OUR HEART HEALER

ARCHANGEL: Chamuel

MEANING OF NAME: "He who sees God"

MAIN ROLE: Heart Healer

SYMBOL: Chalice

COLOR: Pastel pink

CALL UPON THE MIRACLE POWER OF ARCHANGEL CHAMUEL TO:

- Receive divine love
- Find love
- Improve an existing relationship
- Bless my birthday

QUICK PRAYER:

Archangel Chamuel, fill my soul with divine love today!

INTRODUCTION
TO ARCHANGEL CHAMUEL

Archangel Chamuel is one of the lesser-known archangels, but this doesn't mean that his role in the spiritual world is any less important. On the contrary, Chamuel is the archangel of divine love, which could well be the strongest force in the universe. It has often been said that God *is* love and that the Godhead has a boundless unconditional love for all creation.

The name Chamuel means "He who sees God," which likely tells us that he is constantly in the presence of that tremendous fountain of love. And as such, he can transfer that love to anyone anywhere in the universe.

This proximity to God's love makes Archangel Chamuel the perfect messenger of divine love.

Chamuel beams a beautiful pastel-pink light and is often depicted holding a chalice. In our mind's eye, we can visualize Archangel Chamuel pouring the compassionate love of God into our hearts—and by that love, our hearts are comforted and healed.

TRUE STORY:
WITHIN 90 DAYS,
MR. RIGHT APPEARED

As a single mother and a lawyer, Sandra was financially secure, lived in a nice house and spent time with friends. But it was tough to be alone and she longed for love in her life.

Sandra went on several dates, but none of them worked out. "I lost my self-confidence, ignored men altogether and gained weight," she said. "And I felt as if that special person who would love me and take care of me just didn't exist."

A few weeks later, a friend introduced Sandra to the archangels and told her to write a letter to Archangel Chamuel, pouring out her feelings, and then to burn the letter.

Sandra's lawyer mind kicked in and she was skeptical at first. But she relented and wrote the letter, expressing her desire for love. Then she burned it, fully expecting nothing to come of this "silly" exercise.

Ninety days passed and nothing happened. Sandra was disappointed and took refuge in comfort food. And then, Mr. Right appeared. His name was Liam and she met him at the library, completely by accident. Or so it seemed.

At first she was nervous and had her doubts. Would this relationship be just a fling? Something to satisfy the burning desire for love, while her soul yearned for a deeper connection?

But as time passed, everything clicked, and she knew Liam was the one she had been waiting for. She knew Liam was Mr. Right.

Sandra and Liam got married twelve months after they met. "I couldn't have asked for more," Sandra said. "I'm really blessed to have found my soulmate. And I'll never forget Archangel Chamuel."

ARCHANGEL CHAMUEL IN OUR LIFE

Archangel Chamuel is our compassionate Heart Healer. He bestows upon us the blessings of better relationships, concern for others and freedom from self-condemnation. What's more, he teaches us that love is the ultimate healing unguent for our souls. When we allow Archangel Chamuel to enfold us in his arms, we experience divine love as a soothing balm that heals our emotional wounds, opening the way to greater possibilities and ultimate joy.

As tender instruments of feeling and caring, our hearts can easily get hurt. When the blows of life land on our hearts, we tend to quickly withdraw our senses from the place of pain, like turtles retreating into their shells. Or, if we are seriously hurt, we may lash out in anger at what we perceive to be the source of that hurt.

Though these responses protect us in the moment, neither withdrawing nor lashing out is healthy in the long run. We can't live with a closed-off heart for too long without getting ill or depressed.

Eventually, we'll have to come back into our hearts and learn to use the power of love for healing, harmony and joy.

And that is when we ask for the help of Archangel Chamuel, our Heart Healer, to mend our broken hearts and heal our emotional wounds so that we are free to experience the inner peace and happiness we seek.

Archangel Chamuel's divine love is different from the common pattern of reciprocal human love. It is a steadily sustained love that flows to us all the time, unconditionally. And this love continues to come to us whether or not we recognize it or feel worthy to receive it.

Let each of us become a deep well of this divine love, pouring it to all unconditionally and, at the same time, blessing ourselves and the world.

PAINTINGS

PAGE 62: Archangel Chamuel with Chalice
PAGE 64: Archangel Chamuel with Ruby Crystal
PAGE 66: Angel of Bliss
PAGE 68: Recording Angel

To see these paintings in color, please go to
HouseOfTheArchangels.com

THIRD SMALL GIFT:
THE SECRET POWER OF LOVE: A FABLE

Deep in the Rocky Mountains, a gold miner named Ralph and his wife, Abby, lead a simple life, until a chance encounter with three trapped fairies changes everything.

Upon being freed by the couple, each of the grateful fairies offers them a unique blessing that will transform their life in remarkable ways. But they can only choose one of their gifts: abundance, success or love. What to do?

Follow the enchanting journey that unfolds in the Rockies, unveiling the secret power of love.

To access this captivating tale, please visit our website at the URL below:

bit.ly/mysevengifts

ARCHANGEL PRAYER
TO RECEIVE DIVINE LOVE

Archangel Chamuel, blessed Heart Healer, servant of the Most High,

In the name I AM THAT I AM, I ask you to enfold me in your arms of love.

Pour divine love into my heart and let me experience God's love for all creation.

Vanquish all forces of anti-love within me until nothing less than love remains, and all is bliss.

Teach me how to magnify this love and share it unconditionally with everyone I meet.

Guide and support me each day.

I thank you for receiving my prayer and for your service to humanity.

And I accept the blessing of divine love, in keeping with my divine plan.

This which I ask for myself, I ask for all beings on planet Earth.

ARCHANGEL PRAYER
TO FIND LOVE

Archangel Chamuel, blessed Heart Healer, servant of the Most High,

In the name I AM THAT I AM, I ask you to help me find love in my life.

Pour divine love into my heart and lead me, unerringly, to the person who is waiting for my love and shares my values and interests.

Free me from poor self-worth, self-doubt and all limitations standing in the way of attracting my soulmate.

Teach me how to feel confident and deserving and to know when my perfect partner has come.

Guide and support me each day.

I thank you for receiving my prayer and for your service to humanity.

And I accept the blessing of finding love, in keeping with my divine plan.

This which I ask for myself, I ask for all beings on planet Earth.

ARCHANGEL PRAYER
TO IMPROVE AN EXISTING RELATIONSHIP

Archangel Chamuel, blessed Heart Healer, servant of the Most High,

In the name I AM THAT I AM, I ask you to help me improve my relationship with _____.

Pour divine love into our hearts and help us take our relationship to a new level of love and connection.

Lift the walls of all judgment, resentment and anger, and strengthen the bond of love between us.

Teach us both to love deeply and unconditionally so that we can thrive together.

Guide and support us each day.

I thank you for receiving my prayer and for your service to humanity.

And I accept the blessing of improving my existing relationship, in keeping with our divine plan.

This which I ask for myself, I ask for all beings on planet Earth.

ARCHANGEL PRAYER TO BLESS MY BIRTHDAY

Archangel Chamuel, blessed Heart Healer, servant of the Most High,

In the name I AM THAT I AM, I ask you to bestow angelic blessings upon me on this auspicious day of my birthday.

Pour divine love into my heart and empower me to fulfill my divine destiny in this life.

Clear me from all limitations that may be blocking my spiritual growth, abundance and joy, and unveil new opportunities that will lead me to my highest purpose.

Teach me how to draw on the infinite reservoir of divine light and fulfill all my dreams, while serving others at the same time.

Guide and support me each day.

I thank you for receiving my prayer and for your service to humanity.

And I accept the blessing of finding love, in keeping with my divine plan.

This which I ask for myself, I ask for all beings on planet Earth.

HOW PEOPLE EXPERIENCE OUR ANGELIC FINE ART

"Thank you for the beautiful art. I feel more love in my heart after viewing these beautiful pictures."

—*Janie*

"Beautiful! Beautiful! Thank you for allowing us to see our sweet archangels. Archangel Chamuel has been a great help in my remembering how to forgive and love."

—*Deana*

"Awe inspiring! Beautiful work! Let us love one another and be the light to our world."

—*Cynthia*

"This art is incredibly uplifting! I can truly sense a profound essence of light and love. Absolutely electrifying!"

—*Jorge*

"I have decorated my house with your paintings. They're so inspirational to everyone who sees them."

—*Andrew*

CHAPTER 6:
ARCHANGEL GABRIEL,
OUR MESSENGER OF HOPE

ARCHANGEL:	Gabriel
MEANING OF NAME:	"God is my strength"
MAIN ROLE:	Messenger of Hope
SYMBOL:	Trumpet or lily
COLOR:	White

**CALL UPON THE MIRACLE POWER
OF ARCHANGEL GABRIEL TO:**

- Have hope
- Express more gratitude
- Receive divine guidance
- Overcome procrastination
- Let go of shame

QUICK PRAYER:

*Archangel Gabriel, kindle the flame
of hope in my heart, now and always!*

INTRODUCTION
TO ARCHANGEL GABRIEL

Gabriel is one of the best-known archangels. He is a powerful spiritual being known for his joy, purity and ability to communicate to us important messages from the Divine.

Archangel Gabriel is often depicted holding a trumpet, a symbol of his role as a herald of good news from above. He is also revered for his ability to help people find strength and courage in challenging times.

Wherever Gabriel appears with his awe-inspiring power and angelic light, he imparts visions and words of hope for a better future. Hope radiates from him as an irresistible force for the better, both for individuals and society at large.

With his uplifting energy, Gabriel brings spiritual renewal. Many find that when they invoke his aid, they feel more optimistic and experience greater clarity and focus, along with a greater ability to move forward with their lives.

This blessed archangel emanates a brilliant white light. His name means "God is my strength."

TRUE STORY:
GRANDPA BRINGS HOPE TO GRANDSON

Grayson had recently lost his graphic design job after a layoff. Having nothing better to do, he visited his grandfather on the other side of Kansas City.

Picking up right away that Grayson needed some comfort, his grandfather decided to help. "I've never told this story to anyone," he said, "not even to your grandmother. But I think it's important for you to hear, because you need to get some hope going in your life right now."

Growing up, Grayson's grandfather lived in an unhappy home. His father was an alcoholic and there were often arguments in the house. To find refuge away from home, his grandfather took up basketball, joined the school team and became a skilled point guard.

During his senior year of high school, he learned that he would not be starting as a point guard for the team. This news, along with his difficult home life, devastated him.

One day, while his grandfather was standing outside the front door of his house, a man approached him. "Something was definitely different about this man," grandfather said. "But I just couldn't put my finger on it." The man told him not to worry and that everything would work out in the end.

After the man spoke to him, his grandfather turned toward

the door of his house for a second, and then looked back to-
ward the man. But he had vanished! Confused, his grandfather
didn't know what to think.

Just then, a car pulled up. It was the basketball coach from
another team in the area, a team that was a class above his
former team. The coach asked him if he would like to be a
point guard for that year's team. Almost speechless, he
accepted the offer.

"I've never talked about this to anyone before you today,
because they'd think I was crazy," grandfather said. "But it
really happened." Maybe the man who told him not to worry
was an angel, and maybe he was not. No matter—he was a
messenger of hope.

ARCHANGEL GABRIEL IN OUR LIFE

Archangel Gabriel is our Messenger of Hope. Out of his great
love for humanity, he delivers to us the graces of discipline,
guidance and joy. He fills us with optimism and upliftment that
propel us forward in ways we may not have experienced before.
When we ask this celestial messenger to enter our worlds, we
know hope as a spiritual embrace that comforts us in times of
struggle, protecting us from the arrows of doubt.

Many situations cause us to lose hope, especially when we
deal with major challenges. When we feel hopeless, discour-

agement creeps into our minds. We believe ourselves defeated and disconnected from the world around us. We think we have no control over our lives, and we fail to reach important goals.

So even though a sense of despair may be hard to avoid when all seems lost, we should resist it and not allow it to sprout in the garden of our consciousness. It's useless to keep dragging ourselves down, feeling despondent and discouraged.

At long last, we must reach deep into our souls, unleash the power of hope and face our challenges head on.

And that is where Archangel Gabriel, our Messenger of Hope, comes to the rescue. With love and gratitude in our hearts, we call upon him to flood us with hope. To give us the strength to persevere, no matter what comes our way. To lift us out of negativity and help us soar to new heights of inspiration and accomplishment.

Archangel Gabriel's hope is not the same as the fleeting moments of positivity that we grab onto with our human minds. It's a deep, abiding hope that flows from the center of the divine presence above. A hope that transforms our despair upon contact. A hope that helps us see the silver lining in every situation and believe that anything is possible.

May we become sowers of this blessed hope—planting seeds of joy and optimism wherever we go, dispelling doom and gloom, and making the world a better place.

PAINTINGS

To see these paintings in color, please go to
HouseOfTheArchangels.com

FOURTH SMALL GIFT:
FIVE TIMELESS LESSONS FROM PLATO

Alithia, the ancient and modern Greek word for "truth," translates in English as "No forgetfulness." For the ancient Greeks, to find truth did not mean to learn per se, but to remember. To remember that which is already known by the soul yet has been forgotten.

In his *Allegory of the Cave,* Plato takes us on a thought-provoking exploration of the human condition. Through this captivating story, he paints a vivid picture of individuals trapped in a world of shadows, challenging us to question the reality we perceive and urging us to seek higher truths. Urging us to remember.

You are welcome to claim your fourth gift and journey to the Platonic cave's depths—where the secrets of five timeless lessons await—by visiting our website at the URL below:

bit.ly/mysevengifts

ARCHANGEL PRAYER
TO HAVE HOPE

Archangel Gabriel, blessed Messenger of Hope, servant of the Most High,

In the name I AM THAT I AM, I ask you to help me believe in a better future.

Beam your ray of hope upon me and fill me with optimism and joy.

Dispel all negativity from my mind, and help me to be strong when the arrows of fear assail me.

Teach me to discern the next steps I must take on the path of life and to trust that all will be well in the end.

Guide and support me each day.

I thank you for receiving my prayer and for your service to humanity.

And I accept the blessing of hope, in keeping with my divine plan.

This which I ask for myself, I ask for all beings on planet Earth.

ARCHANGEL PRAYER
TO EXPRESS MORE GRATITUDE

Archangel Gabriel, blessed Messenger of Hope, servant of the Most High,

In the name I AM THAT I AM, I ask you to help me experience and express a deep feeling of gratitude.

Beam your ray of hope upon me and inspire me to appreciate all blessings in my life, both great and small.

Take the weight of ingratitude from my heart, and empower me to cultivate thankfulness toward the Divine, my family and all people in my life.

Teach me to focus on the positive instead of the negative so that I always have an attitude of optimism, gratitude and joy.

Guide and support me each day.

I thank you for receiving my prayer and for your service to humanity.

And I accept the blessing of expressing more gratitude, in keeping with my divine plan.

This which I ask for myself, I ask for all beings on planet Earth.

ARCHANGEL PRAYER
TO RECEIVE DIVINE GUIDANCE

Archangel Gabriel, blessed Messenger of Hope, servant of the Most High,

In the name I AM THAT I AM, I ask you to help me receive divine guidance, especially in regard to

_____.

Beam your ray of hope upon me and reveal to me the next steps on my life's journey.

Banish all fear, lack of faith and attachment to preferred outcomes, and allow me to perceive direction from above with an open mind and heart.

Teach me to have discernment and recognize the still small voice within and to muster the courage to act on the guidance I am given.

Guide and support me each day.

I thank you for receiving my prayer and for your service to humanity.

And I accept the blessing of receiving guidance, in keeping with my divine plan.

This which I ask for myself, I ask for all beings on planet Earth.

ARCHANGEL PRAYER
TO OVERCOME PROCRASTINATION

Archangel Gabriel, blessed Messenger of Hope, servant of the Most High,

In the name I AM THAT I AM, I ask you to help me overcome procrastination.

Beam your ray of hope upon me and grant me the ability to be disciplined and proactive.

Root out the inner causes behind my procrastination, including fear of failure and the desire for instant gratification, and empower me to take timely action.

Teach me how to work on my tasks when they need to get done and not put them off, and how to stick to realistic timelines without feeling overwhelmed or stressed out.

Guide and support me each day.

I thank you for receiving my prayer and for your service to humanity.

And I accept the blessing of overcoming procrastination, in keeping with my divine plan.

This which I ask for myself, I ask for all beings on planet Earth.

ARCHANGEL PRAYER
TO LET GO OF SHAME

Archangel Gabriel, blessed Messenger of Hope, servant of the Most High,

In the name I AM THAT I AM, I ask you to help me let go of the shame that I carry deep within.

Beam your ray of hope upon me and give me sanctuary in your angelic arms, where I can find solace and love.

Cast out the gloom of guilt, self-condemnation and humiliation, and restore my wholeness.

Teach me how to forgive myself, despite the mistakes of the past, and how to rediscover my self-worth and dignity.

Guide and support me each day.

I thank you for receiving my prayer and for your service to humanity.

And I accept the blessing of letting go of shame, in keeping with my divine plan.

This which I ask for myself, I ask for all beings on planet Earth.

HOW PEOPLE EXPERIENCE OUR ANGELIC FINE ART

"I love your angel creations and exquisite representation of the heavenly worlds. They transformed my house into a heavenly temple. Please continue to bring heaven on earth!"

—*Andrei*

"I cried after an hour of sitting and looking at your work. Thank you for your dedication and the incredible beauty."

—*Christine*

"These paintings of angels are the most beautiful I've ever seen, and they radiate so much light and love. When people see them in my home, they comment on their beauty."

—*Diane*

"I don't remember how I came across your most inspiring paintings, but I do know what pure joy and beauty they bring to my world. The connection I have with these beautiful pics is just pure joy and such a blessing."

—*Annemarie*

"Looking at your paintings transports me to a high vibration, where I am lifted out of the humdrum into the Divine."

—*Lynette*

CHAPTER 7:
ARCHANGEL RAPHAEL,
OUR DIVINE PHYSICIAN

ARCHANGEL:	Raphael
MEANING OF NAME:	"God has healed"
MAIN ROLE:	Divine Physician
SYMBOL:	Staff
COLOR:	Emerald green

CALL UPON THE MIRACLE POWER OF ARCHANGEL RAPHAEL TO:

- Receive healing
- Work through grief
- Increase abundance
- Develop a healing presence
- Improve my work life

QUICK PRAYER:

Archangel Raphael, make me whole!

INTRODUCTION
TO ARCHANGEL RAPHAEL

Revered for his ability to bring about physical, emotional and spiritual healing, Archangel Raphael is a beloved figure among many spiritual seekers. Along with Gabriel and Michael, he is one of the best-known archangels.

Archangel Raphael emits a beautiful emerald-green light and is often depicted holding a staff or a wand, symbolizing his role as a healer and a guide. His name means "God has healed" and can also be translated as "Medicine of God." Although Raphael is known as the archangel of healing, his gifts extend well beyond physical healing. He grants us a vision of wholeness at many levels of our being—body, mind and soul.

Archangel Raphael knows that the absence of wholeness ultimately stems from having neglected or lost the connection to our spiritual source. Physical problems, lack of abundance and unfulfilling relationships are often a reflection of this lost inner connection.

One of the key blessings that Archangel Raphael can bestow upon us is to help us discover where we have left off on our spiritual journey. He can guide us in restoring our vision and clarity of purpose, and show us the healing that must take place to renew our relationship with the Divine and with our fellow human beings.

TRUE STORY:
THE MIRACLE HANDS OF AN ANGEL SURGEON

Oscar was driving Marla home after a visit to the hospital, where she had undergone surgery for a torn shoulder muscle. Halfway home, Marla complained that the painkillers weren't working, and the pain had become too much to bear.

"Archangel Raphael, help Marla right now!" Oscar said without thinking much, his voice booming in their Ford Explorer SUV. Both Oscar and Marla had worked with the archangels before, and Marla taught classes about the archangels at her yoga studio.

Within seconds, Oscar felt a strong tingle within his heart. Trying not to take his eyes off the road for too long, he turned to Marla and saw an angel sewing her torn muscle with a needle and green thread.

Oscar rubbed his eyes to make sure he wasn't hallucinating, looked away and then back at Marla. But the angel was still there. He finished sewing the torn muscle across her shoulder and then vanished.

Almost immediately, Marla's pain subsided. The doctor had told them that the pain would last for several weeks, but it was gone within just 48 hours. "I couldn't believe how quickly Marla's pain went away," Oscar said. "I expected some help, for sure. But not so quickly. I love getting surprised by the angels!"

ARCHANGEL RAPHAEL IN OUR LIFE

Archangel Raphael is our Divine Physician. In addition to healing, he endows us with spiritual sight, abundance and truth. When we petition this blessed being to come to our aid, we realize that he not only helps us with our requests, but also offers us an all-encompassing state of wholeness. Wholeness that, like a key, liberates us from the prison of suffering, opening the door to harmony, balance and unity.

Despite the universal desire to always be healthy, people of all ages struggle with health challenges. Beyond physical pain or limitations imposed by our condition, poor health often makes us feel trapped in a cycle of emotional suffering, as if we are carrying a heavy burden that we can never fully let go of. We may also fall into fear and uncertainty about our future.

When we experience such circumstances, it may be tempting to simply give up and accept our lot in life. Yet, it is precisely at this moment of falling into a downward spiral of negative thoughts and emotions that we must remember that with God, all things are possible. It is in this moment of deep anguish that we must summon angelic help.

THE MIRACLE POWER OF THE ARCHANGELS

And that is when Archangel Raphael—the Divine Physician of body, mind and soul—steps through the veil to help us navigate through these emotional and physical challenges. To show us the light at the end of the proverbial tunnel. To comfort us and beam his ray of healing upon us. To restore wholeness to our wounded souls.

When we ask for healing, we must do so in the spirit of surrender, knowing that Archangel Raphael will surely answer our prayers, even if things don't turn out exactly the way we had expected. We can rest assured that the solution will be for our highest good, in keeping with our divine plan and any lessons that we need to learn from our state of dis-ease. It is important, of course, to heed our doctor's advice, while at the same time pursuing the natural healing modalities at our disposal.

So let us welcome the gift of divine wholeness into our lives today and allow Archangel Raphael's holy presence to guide us through our trials with clarity and determination.

May we become emissaries of that wholeness, healing the scars of our past, overcoming the obstacles of today, finding inner peace and sharing it with everyone around us. Together, we can.

PAINTINGS

To see these paintings in color, please go to
HouseOfTheArchangels.com

FIFTH SMALL GIFT:
ABUNDANCE & SUBCONSCIOUS SABOTEURS

Abundance is usually defined as money in the bank, investments and assets. In its highest form, abundance also represents the divine flow of energy that brings us the spiritual blessings and economic prosperity we need to realize our unique destiny.

Sometimes, despite our best efforts, creating a flow of more abundance in our life seems blocked. We sense something is off, yet we can't pin down the exact cause. One reason may be that, deep down, there is hidden resistance. Deep down, we may not feel we deserve more abundance. Deep down, we are allowing our subconscious saboteurs to create another reality.

Your fifth gift will help you discover these subconscious saboteurs and show you how to transform them. To access it, please visit our website at the URL below:

bit.ly/mysevengifts

ARCHANGEL PRAYER TO RECEIVE HEALING

Archangel Raphael, blessed Divine Physician, servant of the Most High,

In the name I AM THAT I AM, I ask you to heal me today.

Place your holy staff over me and beam your ray of wholeness into my heart. Remove all blocks to my perfect recovery, and bring balance to my physical, emotional and spiritual bodies.

Teach me the lesson behind this illness, and grant me the strength I need to face my situation with grace.

Guide and support me each day.

I thank you for receiving my prayer and for your service to humanity.

And I accept the blessing of healing, in keeping with my divine plan.

This which I ask for myself, I ask for all beings on planet Earth.

ARCHANGEL PRAYER
TO WORK THROUGH GRIEF

Archangel Raphael, blessed Divine Physician, servant of the Most High,

In the name I AM THAT I AM, I ask you to help me work through my grief.

Place your holy staff over me and mend the hole in my heart.

Part the clouds of darkness and despair, and give me refuge in your divine embrace.

Teach me how to traverse this dark passage, releasing all sorrow as I emerge into the light of peace.

Guide and support me each day.

I thank you for receiving my prayer and for your service to humanity.

And I accept the blessing of working through my grief, in keeping with my divine plan.

This which I ask for myself, I ask for all beings on planet Earth.

ARCHANGEL PRAYER
TO INCREASE ABUNDANCE

Archangel Raphael, blessed Divine Physician, servant of the Most High,

In the name I AM THAT I AM, I ask you to help me increase the abundance in my life, especially in the area of _____.

Place your holy staff over me and infuse me with a sense of limitless abundance and infinite possibilities.

Dissolve all limiting beliefs that are blocking the flow of the abundance I seek, and reveal the opportunities before me that align with my highest good.

Teach me how to attract all the money, wealth and resources I need to fulfill my goals, serve others and contribute to worthy causes.

Guide and support me each day.

I thank you for receiving my prayer and for your service to humanity.

And I accept the blessing of increasing my abundance, in keeping with my divine plan.

This which I ask for myself, I ask for all beings on planet Earth.

ARCHANGEL PRAYER TO DEVELOP A HEALING PRESENCE

Archangel Raphael, blessed Divine Physician, servant of the Most High,

In the name I AM THAT I AM, I ask you to help me develop a healing presence.

Place your holy staff over me and endow me with your regenerative divine power.

Deliver me from human limitations and bond me to your heart so I can bring comfort, love and wholeness to all who are in my care.

Teach me how to stay centered and strong and assist those in need even in the face of adversity.

Guide and support me each day.

I thank you for receiving my prayer and for your service to humanity.

And I accept the blessing of developing a healing presence, in keeping with my divine plan.

This which I ask for myself, I ask for all beings on planet Earth.

ARCHANGEL PRAYER
TO IMPROVE MY WORK LIFE

Archangel Raphael, blessed Divine Physician, servant of the Most High,

In the name I AM THAT I AM, I ask you to help me improve my work life.

Place your holy staff over me and beam your emerald-green ray of healing and abundance into my workplace.

Clear all obstacles that stand in the way of harmonious cooperation, and empower me, my colleagues and superiors to build the best possible work environment to benefit and uplift everyone involved.

Teach me how to have a successful career and how to find joy and fulfillment in my daily work.

Guide and support me each day.

I thank you for receiving my prayer and for your service to humanity.

And I accept the blessing of improving my work life, in keeping with my divine plan.

This which I ask for myself, I ask for all beings on planet Earth.

HOW PEOPLE EXPERIENCE OUR ANGELIC FINE ART

"I had been searching for a long time for some beautiful angel pictures. At a friend's healing practice, I noticed she had three beautifully framed paintings by you. Since that time eight years ago, I have gathered a wonderful collection in my own healing practice, and they never fail to inspire and comfort my patients. Your work touches people's souls and allows them to heal."

—*Elizabeth Anne*

"Your beautiful paintings fill me with so much love that tears stream from my eyes. It is the spiritual connecting that is at the heart of every one of your paintings."

—*Carol Anne*

"I admire your wonderful and beautiful heavenly works. They are just breathtaking, and there are absolutely no words to describe these miracle art works. It looks like heaven is here on earth and our questions are just about to be answered."

—*Diana*

"The paintings are just incredibly beautiful and healing. So absolutely gorgeous that anyone who spends time looking at any of them will be uplifted."

—*Angela*

CHAPTER 8:
ARCHANGEL URIEL,
OUR PATRON OF PEACE

ARCHANGEL:	Uriel
MEANING OF NAME:	"God is my light"
MAIN ROLE:	Patron of Peace
SYMBOL:	Book or scroll
COLOR:	Purple and gold

**CALL UPON THE MIRACLE POWER
OF ARCHANGEL URIEL TO:**

- Find peace
- Manage stress
- Overcome anger
- Have patience
- Increase motivation

QUICK PRAYER:

Archangel Uriel, bless me with the gift of peace today!

INTRODUCTION
TO ARCHANGEL URIEL

Though he is one of the lesser-known archangels, Uriel is a key archangel to know and work with. Often depicted holding a book or a scroll, symbolizing his role as teacher and guide, Archangel Uriel radiates a shimmering purple and golden light.

His name means "God is my light" or "God is my flame," and he wields this light and flame in two different areas of service.

First, Uriel focuses his powerful influence and action in the areas of divine justice and righteousness. He goes to work against injustice wherever it is found, whether in the courtrooms of the world or in relationships between individuals, communities and nations.

At the same time, Uriel is also the archangel of peace and brotherhood. He and his legions of angels promote tolerance, camaraderie and participation in any type of selfless service that helps those in need.

Archangel Uriel is mentioned in some spiritual traditions, where he is often seen as the keeper of beauty and light, as well as the regent of the sun.

TRUE STORY:
THE LOST WEDDING RING

Owen worked as a welder at the local factory. After taking a break in the factory's garden and returning to his post, he realized he had lost his wedding ring.

Determined to find it, he retraced his steps in the garden. He looked everywhere—twice—but nothing. The ring had vanished, seemingly in thin air. "What am I going to tell Ava?" he thought to himself. "She won't be happy."

Owen decided to keep it a secret for now and to look for the ring again the next day. During the evening, Ava didn't notice the missing ring—as if an unseen power was "protecting" him.

Right before he went to bed, Owen felt a prompting to ask the angels to help him out. He also asked the angel of peace to keep him and Ava calm and collected the next day, just in case he didn't find the ring and he had to break the news to her.

The next morning, Owen went back to work. As soon as he reached his station, he saw a little pouch sitting on his work-table. Grabbing the pouch, he felt a warm sensation come over him. Inside was his wedding ring!

"I don't know if the factory workers on the night shift found my ring and put it on my desk," Owen said, "because no one came forward to speak about it. And I can't prove it was the angels who guided someone to the ring, but who knows? Whoever brought me the ring literally saved me!"

ARCHANGEL URIEL IN OUR LIFE

Archangel Uriel is our Patron of Peace. He imparts to us the boons of inner peace, patience, relief from stress, freedom from anger and the inspiration to selflessly serve humanity. When we invoke the holy presence of Archangel Uriel, we perceive peace as a flowing river that carries away our pain, restoring our souls to their pure estate.

In a world that often feels chaotic and unpredictable, it's easy to get caught up in turmoil and lose our sense of peace. Our minds get overwhelmed, making us unable to stay present and mindful. The pressures of work, relationships and finances can cause us to feel stressed, leading to anxiety, depression and even physical illness.

In such moments of intense pressure, we may drop into a "fight response," lashing out at others in frustration and anger, sabotaging the very relationships we need for our support. Or we may adopt a "flight response," thinking that running away from a situation will cause our problem to disappear. We may even have a "freeze response," reacting like the typical deer in the headlights, becoming virtually incapacitated, unable to make a move to resolve the situation.

Although these instinctive responses may provide temporary relief and appear to solve our problems in the short run, they don't lead to a sustainable solution. Aggression and avoidance can lead to further suffering and isolation, making our situation even worse.

In due time, we must find a way to harness the power of divine peace and get our emotions under control so we can respond to our challenges with courage and equanimity.

And that is where Archangel Uriel, our Patron of Peace, comes to offer his support and deliver us from the forces of anti-peace. To comfort us and minister to our needs. To draw us into the furnace of his loving heart and melt away our anger and frustration. To bring us the serenity and guidance we need to weather even our most turbulent personal storms.

The divine peace Archangel Uriel brings to us is not simply the absence of conflict or stress, and it's different from the transitory calmness we may experience from time to time. Instead, it's a state of being in which we feel completely held and supported by a higher power, knowing that we are not alone in our struggles, and that all will be well.

So let us tap into this divine peace and face any challenge that comes our way with grace and equanimity. And let us remember that peace is not a distant dream, but a present reality that we can cultivate today, one archangel prayer at a time.

May we become ambassadors of peace, holding our center and living in the now, guiding our families, our communities and the world toward a brighter, more peaceful future.

PAINTINGS

To see these paintings in color, please go to
HouseOfTheArchangels.com

SIXTH SMALL GIFT:
DISCOVERING A PRIMAL SECRET WITH A LITTLE HELP FROM NATURE

One day, while gazing at the mountain from my door window, I noticed a big spider crawling down the glass. Instinctively, I opened and shut the door to get rid of it.

Opening the door again to see what had happened, to my surprise, the spider was clinging to the door handle. I grabbed an old broom, intending to help it onto the bristles and release it in a nearby bush.

As I reached out, the spider lunged toward the ground with lightning speed, escaping away from the house. Instinctively, I blocked its path with the broom. This was war...

To read the rest of this true story and discover the primal secret the spider unveiled, please visit our website at the URL below:

bit.ly/mysevengifts

ARCHANGEL PRAYER
TO FIND PEACE

Archangel Uriel, blessed Patron of Peace, servant of the Most High,

In the name I AM THAT I AM, I ask you to help me attain a state of serenity.

Enfold me in your wings of peace and enable me to master my emotions.

Vanquish all forces of anti-peace in my world, and empower me to find inner calm.

Teach me to respond to all challenges with equanimity and to not overreact when things don't go the way I expected.

Guide and support me each day.

I thank you for receiving my prayer and for your service to humanity.

And I accept the blessing of peace, in keeping with my divine plan.

This which I ask for myself, I ask for all beings on planet Earth.

ARCHANGEL PRAYER TO MANAGE STRESS

Archangel Uriel, blessed Patron of Peace, servant of the Most High,

In the name I AM THAT I AM, I ask you to help me manage stress.

Enfold me in your wings of peace and open my mind to a more calm and positive outlook.

Liberate me from the chains of all thoughts, feelings and habits that are making me anxious, and fill me with your divine serenity.

Teach me how to cultivate a deep sense of inner peace and have faith that everything will work out for the best even when I'm not in control of a situation.

Guide and support me each day.

I thank you for receiving my prayer and for your service to humanity.

And I accept the blessing of gracefully managing stress, in keeping with my divine plan.

This which I ask for myself, I ask for all beings on planet Earth.

ARCHANGEL PRAYER
TO OVERCOME ANGER

Archangel Uriel, blessed Patron of Peace, servant of the Most High,

In the name I AM THAT I AM, I ask you to help me overcome anger.

Enfold me in your wings of peace and take command of my tendency to have outbursts.

Set me free from the prison of judgment, resentment and retaliation, and empower me to find inner calm.

Teach me how to respond peacefully in situations that may trigger my anger, and show me a better way forward for myself and all involved.

Guide and support me each day.

I thank you for receiving my prayer and for your service to humanity.

And I accept the blessing of overcoming anger, in keeping with my divine plan.

This which I ask for myself, I ask for all beings on planet Earth.

ARCHANGEL PRAYER
TO HAVE PATIENCE

Archangel Uriel, blessed Patron of Peace, servant of the Most High,

In the name I AM THAT I AM, I ask you to help me have more patience.

Enfold me in your wings of peace and endow me with forbearance and equanimity.

Lift the burden of impatience from my shoulders, and empower me to navigate all situations in my life with ease and grace.

Teach me how to overcome the need for instant results, and show me how to become resilient in the face of slow progress.

I thank you for receiving my prayer and for your service to humanity.

And I accept the blessing of having more patience, in keeping with my divine plan.

This which I ask for myself, I ask for all beings on planet Earth.

ARCHANGEL PRAYER
TO INCREASE MOTIVATION

Archangel Uriel, blessed Patron of Peace, servant of the Most High,

In the name I AM THAT I AM, I ask you to help me increase my motivation.

Enfold me in your wings of peace and unleash the power of enthusiasm in my world.

Silence the voices of self-criticism, doubt and discouragement, and flood me with excitement, renewed energy and zeal.

Teach me how to tap into the wellspring of divine inspiration and how to stay positive and strong when I face the ups and downs of life.

Guide and support me each day.

I thank you for receiving my prayer and for your service to humanity.

And I accept the blessing of increasing my motivation, in keeping with my divine plan.

This which I ask for myself, I ask for all beings on planet Earth.

How People Experience Our Angelic Fine Art

"Thank you for the beautiful artwork. My heart took flight as I browsed through the beautiful colors. Before I knew it, I was in tears. The colors you use are so beautiful and uplifting, words can't describe the effect this has on the heart."

—*Anna*

"I have many of your prints in my home; their eyes and faces remind me of Home. The comfort and peace in their expressions manifest goodness all around them."

—*Gladys*

"These beautiful pieces of art in my home and office have inspired me to continue to be of service. A great sense of peace comes over me when I look at them."

—*Brigida*

"Your images have allowed me a visual and more personal experience in my interaction with the higher realms. Extraordinary beauty and life. It has made a huge impact on me."

—*Elle*

"Over the years, I have collected many of your paintings. Their radiance and beauty always give me an uplift."

— *Patrick*

CHAPTER 9:
ARCHANGEL ZADKIEL,
OUR DIVINE LIBERATOR

ARCHANGEL:	Zadkiel
MEANING OF NAME:	"God is my righteousness"
MAIN ROLE:	Divine Liberator
SYMBOL:	Violet fire
COLOR:	Violet

**CALL UPON THE MIRACLE POWER
OF ARCHANGEL ZADKIEL TO:**

- Extend forgiveness
- Transform emotional pain
- Feel happy
- Embrace change

QUICK PRAYER:

*Archangel Zadkiel, saturate my being
with boundless forgiveness right now!*

INTRODUCTION
TO ARCHANGEL ZADKIEL

Archangel Zadkiel, whose name means "God is my right-eousness," is known for empowering spiritual seekers to attain freedom from all limitation, the ultimate blessing. This great celestial being is also revered for his ability to inspire tolerance, facilitate diplomacy and heal rifts among opposing groups of people.

Archangel Zadkiel brings positive change and upliftment with his radiant violet fire, which is also his symbol. Many spiritual seekers discover that in answer to their prayers to him for help, they feel comforted, become free from the effects of emotional trauma and experience spiritual bliss.

Archangel Zadkiel is associated with the mysterious Order of Melchizedek, as well as with alchemy. Unlike the alchemists of old who sought to change the base metal lead into gold, modern alchemists strive to transmute the lead of the human consciousness into the gold of the spirit, with the help of Archangel Zadkiel.

In some traditions, Archangel Zadkiel is considered to be the angel of benevolence, mercy and memory, and is recognized as the angel who held back Abraham's hand when he was about to sacrifice his son Isaac.

TRUE STORY:
DISSOLVING MEMORIES
OF TRAUMA

Jasmine's life changed forever when her son was taken from her too soon. At just seventeen years old, Brayton was fatally caught in the crossfire of street violence in Baltimore. Jasmine, a single mother, was left alone to navigate the overwhelming grief and trauma that came with such a devastating loss.

"I couldn't sleep at night," she said. "The memories of that day kept playing over and over in my head, and I felt as if I was reliving the trauma every time I closed my eyes."

Desperate to find some sense of peace and escape the pain and grief that consumed her, Jasmine turned to the archangels for help. She called upon the mercy of Archangel Zadkiel, imploring him to guide her through the process of emotional recovery and to help her let go of the pain that at times overtook her.

With Zadkiel's sacred energy of forgiveness and transformation, Jasmine began her journey toward healing and found herself able to sleep more peacefully. "I feel like much of the trauma I experienced has been released," she said, "and that even my brain was rewired to give me a more positive perspective on life."

It wasn't an easy process, and many setbacks came along the way. Yet, with the help of Archangel Zadkiel, Jasmine found a sense of peace and acceptance that had previously seemed unattainable.

"I am so grateful to Archangel Zadkiel for helping me through this difficult time," Jasmine says. "I feel I've been able to overcome this difficult event and move forward with my life."

ARCHANGEL ZADKIEL IN OUR LIFE

Archangel Zadkiel is our Divine Liberator. He shares with us the spiritual favors of mercy, change and transmutation of painful memories. When we enlist the assistance of this great being of light, we understand forgiveness as an alchemical elixir that transforms our negative emotions, opening our hearts to healing and grace.

Many times, we find it difficult to forgive others who have hurt us, especially in grievous situations such as betrayal and abuse. Instead of letting go, we hold onto grudges, believing we are justified in our resentment. We may feel like victims, constantly reliving past traumas and blaming others for our pain. We may even stop trusting other people, building walls around ourselves to protect us from further harm. Eventually, we become trapped in a cycle of bitterness that drains our energy and joy.

It's not that we are bad people if we struggle and can't quite bring ourselves to forgive. Yet failing to do so will only lead to more pain and suffering.

This state of turmoil is not the way we are meant to experience life. We are meant to thrive, to grow, to love.

Sooner or later, we must reach deep into our souls to muster the will to change and liberate the power of forgiveness.

And that is where Archangel Zadkiel, our Divine Liberator, enters our personal world to give us the strength to let go of our pain. To help us reconcile our past. To transmute our burdens into light. To free us from all limitation and help us move forward with renewed inspiration and inner wholeness.

Archangel Zadkiel's angelic forgiveness is more than what we typically consider as forgiveness in human terms. Much more than just saying "I'm sorry." It's a divine power, imbued with compassion—a ray of freedom that unshackles us from the chains of the past and opens us up to new possibilities.

So let us experience the joy that comes from embracing this gift of divine forgiveness and become sunbeams of mercy, shining it freely upon all life to break down the walls of division and make the world a more loving and forgiving place.

Paintings

To see these paintings in color, please go to
HouseOfTheArchangels.com

Seventh Small Gift:
THREE FABLES FOR YOUR INNER CHILD

This delightful trio of enchanting fables is bound to reignite the magic of storytelling in your heart and transport your inner child to a place of wonder and wisdom.

Written by the author of this book, each of these stories carries a powerful message that will comfort you and encourage you to never give up:

- *The Story of Emile—The Cobbler Who Learned to Believe in Miracles*
- *The Great Secret of the Butterflies*
- *Princess Evanthe Chooses a Husband*

To access these must-read fables, your seventh small gift, please visit our website at the URL below:

bit.ly/mysevengifts

ARCHANGEL PRAYER
TO EXTEND FORGIVENESS

Archangel Zadkiel, blessed Divine Liberator of all souls, servant of the Most High,

In the name I AM THAT I AM, I ask you to help me forgive myself, my family and everyone who has ever wronged me, especially _____.

Beam your ray of freedom upon me and grant me safe haven in your merciful heart.

Transform all anger, bitterness and past hurts within my being, and show me how to cultivate an attitude of compassion and goodwill.

Teach me to access my inner strength, and empower me to move forward on my life's journey with joy and peace.

Guide and support me each day.

I thank you for receiving my prayer and for your service to humanity.

And I accept the blessing of forgiveness, in keeping with my divine plan.

This which I ask for myself, I ask for all beings on planet Earth.

Archangel Prayer
to Transform Emotional Pain

Archangel Zadkiel, blessed Divine Liberator of all souls, servant of the Most High,

In the name I AM THAT I AM, I ask you to help me transform my deep emotional pain, especially

_____.

Beam your ray of freedom upon me and shelter me in your loving embrace, where I can find comfort and peace.

Quell the storm of anguish, sadness and grief raging within my being, and dissolve all painful memories of trauma once and for all.

Teach me the lessons I must learn, and show me how to use these new insights as guideposts in the journey of self-discovery and growth.

Guide and support me each day.

I thank you for receiving my prayer and for your service to humanity.

And I accept the blessing of transforming my emotional pain, in keeping with my divine plan.

This which I ask for myself, I ask for all beings on planet Earth.

ARCHANGEL PRAYER
TO FEEL HAPPY

Archangel Zadkiel, blessed Divine Liberator of all souls, servant of the Most High,

In the name I AM THAT I AM, I ask you to help me feel more happy.

Beam your ray of freedom upon me and open the door of my mind to a more cheerful and hopeful outlook.

Take away the burden of unhappiness from my heart, and fill me with contentment and divine joy.

Teach me to appreciate my relationships, my work and my daily life, and make me a beacon of happiness to everyone I meet.

Guide and support me each day.

I thank you for receiving my prayer and for your service to humanity.

And I accept the blessing of feeling happy, in keeping with my divine plan.

This which I ask for myself, I ask for all beings on planet Earth.

ARCHANGEL PRAYER TO EMBRACE CHANGE

Archangel Zadkiel, blessed Divine Liberator of all souls, servant of the Most High,

In the name I AM THAT I AM, I ask you to help me embrace the changes that life brings, especially

_____.

Beam your ray of freedom upon me, and empower me to tackle this change with resilience and strength.

Release me from all resistance to the necessary changes in my life, and grant me the courage to step out of my comfort zone and explore new possibilities.

Teach me how to draw upon my inner fortitude, and inspire me to discover new opportunities that will fulfill my dreams in due time.

Guide and support me each day.

I thank you for receiving my prayer and for your service to humanity.

And I accept the blessing of embracing change, in keeping with my divine plan.

This which I ask for myself, I ask for all beings on planet Earth.

How People Experience Our Angelic Fine Art

"I can't tell you how much inspiration and beauty your artwork has brought to my life. I have your images surrounding my altar. They are all so beautiful and open my heart beyond any words!"

—*Deborah*

"I love your extraordinary creations. I feel transported into a luminous world of beauty, love and light."

—*Ronaldo*

"Every home needs these paintings. They're like stepping through portals into heavenly realms."

—*Sheryl*

"I absolutely love your art and have for quite some time. Thank you for the luminous beauty that you create in your art. You truly emulate the glorious radiance of our great heavenly Hosts of Light!"

—*Iolani*

"Your paintings take to me heaven and keep me there. I hope to have your entire collection one day."

—*Dionne*

EPILOGUE

Friendship with an archangel is one of the most precious relationships we can have in our life. As in all relationships, forming a meaningful connection with an archangel goes through stages. It begins with attention on our part, and in time it can develop into mutual love, trust and commitment.

The more our relationships with the archangels grow, the more our consciousness will expand, enabling us to magnetize and radiate more of their divine energies. Which means we can give greater service to our families and the world.

Please keep in mind that these mighty archangels desire deeply to help mankind in any way they can. And that they are very grateful when those of us on earth call them into action.

So we encourage you to work with the archangels today. To ask for and receive the blessings that they are ready to bestow upon you and the world. The time to believe in the miracle power of the archangels and to quickly unleash it is *now*.

Continue the Journey...

To continue your journey into the world of the arch-angels, we invite you to join our newsletter community and gain access to a wealth of insights, stories and helpful guidance.

Plus, you'll be the first to know about exclusive offers on our archangel prints and products.

To sign up, please visit our website:
HouseOfTheArchangels.com

DON'T FORGET YOUR SMALL GIFTS

- From Negative Self-Talk to Empowerment (pg. 25)
- The Greatest Theft of All Ages (pg. 43)
- The Secret Power of Love: A Fable (pg. 61)
- Five Timeless Lessons from Plato (pg. 77)
- Abundance & Subconscious Saboteurs (pg. 95)
- Discovering a Primal Secret (pg. 113)
- Three Fables for Your Inner Child (pg. 131)

To access your small gifts,
please visit our website:
<u>bit.ly/mysevengifts</u>

About
the House of the Archangels

The archangels are powerful spiritual beings who are always ready to help us solve our problems and grant us divine gifts. At the House of the Archangels, our mission is to spread greater awareness of these magnificent beings and bring them into the lives of millions. We believe that as more people ask for the archangels' blessings and empower them to act in their world, this divine exchange will benefit not only themselves but also their families, their communities and the world at large. To facilitate this spiritual connection, we offer a variety of archangel-focused resources, including fine art, books, products and education.

About the Author

George Makris is a visionary self-help author who teaches people how to create small miracles in their lives by tapping into the power of the archangels. He also serves as an executive advisor to CEOs in the health, wellness and nonprofit industries. George moved to America from Cyprus after winning a college scholarship and has lived there ever since. Along with Marius Michael-George, he is the co-founder of House of the Archangels, an organization dedicated to spreading greater awareness of the archangels and bringing them into the lives of millions. George is an eternal optimist who believes in a better tomorrow. His upcoming books include *You Can Live Longer and Better: A Holistic Approach* and *The Greatest Secret of All Ages: A Spiritual Adventure.*

ABOUT THE ARTIST

Marius Michael-George is a classically trained visionary artist and art teacher. Through his art, he seeks to inspire people and open portals to higher realms. Marius came to America from Bucharest, Romania, as a young artist. Today, he resides and creates his art in Paradise Valley, Montana. Marius studied with Frank Mason at the Art Students League in New York City and was also trained in the system of classical realism at Atelier LeSueur and Atelier Lack in Minneapolis. His original oil paintings and murals are found in public and private collections across North and South America, Australia and Europe and all artwork is published internationally as prints and cards. Marius' art is represented by numerous international publishers, including Hay House Inc., Leanin' Tree, Doreen Virtue Oracle Cards, Ullstein Verlag, Wrage GmbH, Amber Lotus, Dynavision Japan and many others.

Bibliography

Fischer, Lynn, *Angels of Love and Light* (South Yarmouth, Massachusetts: Transformational Media Publications, 1996)

Hopkins, Emma Curtis, *High Mysticism* (Vancouver, Washington: Wise Woman Press, 2012)

Jones, David Albert, *Angels: A Very Short Introduction* (Oxford, United Kingdom: Oxford University Press, 2011)

Marshall, George, *Angels: An Indexed and Partially Annotated Bibliography of over 4300 Scholarly Books and Articles Since the 7th Century B.C.* (Jefferson, North Carolina: McFarland Publishing, 1999)

Miller, Stephen, *The Book of Angels* (Newcastle upon Tyne, United Kingdom: Cambridge Scholars Publishing, 2019)

Mother Alexandra, *The Holy Angels* (Chesterton, Indiana: Ancient Faith Publishing, 2019)

Pagels, Elaine, *The Gnostic Gospels* (New York, New York: Random House, 1989)

Prophet, Elizabeth Clare, *How to Work with Angels* (Gardiner, Montana: Summit University Press, 1989)

Pseudo-Dionysius the Areopagite, *The Celestial Hierarchy* (Whitefish, Montana: Kessinger Publishing, 2010)

Scofield, Cyrus Ingerson, *The New Scofield Study Bible, New King James Version* (Nashville, Tennessee: Thomas Nelson, 1989)

Swedenborg, Emanuel, *Angelic Wisdom Concerning the Divine Love and the Divine Wisdom* (Katy, Texas: Cornerstone Book Publishers, 2010)

Thank you for reading
The Miracle Power of the Archangels!

If you enjoyed the book,
please consider leaving a review
on Amazon.

Printed in Great Britain
by Amazon